Quick Tips

Guitar Technique 101

Don J. MacLean

© Copyright 2004, Don J. MacLean.

Printed and Bound in Canada. All Rights Reserved. International Copyright Secured.

No part of this book may be reproduced or transmitted in any form or by any means, mechanical or electronic, including photocopying, recording, or by information storage and retrieval system—except by a reviewer who may quote brief passages in a review to be printed in a magazine or newspaper—without permission in writing from the publisher. For information, please contact Agogic Publishing 406-109 Tenth Street, New Westminster, British Columbia, V3M 3X7.

Text editing: Jeneane McKenzie
Photography: Michael Rafter

National Library of Canada Cataloguing in Publication Data

MacLean, Don J., 1968-
  Quick tips : guitar technique 101 / Don J. MacLean ; Jeneane McKenzie, editor.

ISBN 1-896595-25-1

1. Guitar--Studies and exercises. I. McKenzie, Jeneane, 1968- II. Title.
MT585.M1622 2003   787.87'193   C2003-911267-5

Quantity discounts are available on bulk purchases of this book for educational purposes. For information please contact Agogic Publishing 406-109 Tenth Street, New Westminster, British Columbia, V3M 3X7, (604) 290-2692.

Visit us on our website:
http://www.agogic.biz
for free downloads
and product information.

Contents

About the Author 1
Introduction 2

Chapter 1 Basics

How to Hold the Guitar 3
How to Hold a Pick 3
Fret-hand Position 5
Music Notation 6
Standard Notation 7
A Quick Overview of Tablature 7

Chapter 2 Rhythm

Meter 8
Time Values 9
Note Durations 9
Rest Durations 10
Time Signatures 10
Dotted and Tied Notes 11
Repeats 12

Chapter 3 How to Practice

How to Practice 13

Chapter 4 Vibrato
Vibrato 15
Vibrato Exercise No. 1 16

Chapter 5 Alternate Picking
Alternate Picking 17
Alternate Picking Exercise No. 1 18
Alternate Picking Exercise No. 2 19
Alternate Picking Exercise No. 3 20
Alternate Picking Exercise No. 4 21
Alternate Picking Exercise No. 5 22
Alternate Picking Exercise No. 6 23
Alternate Picking Exercise No. 7 24
Alternate Picking Exercise No. 8 24
Alternate Picking Exercise No. 9 25
Alternate Picking Exercise No. 10 25
Alternate Picking Exercise No. 11 26
Alternate Picking Exercise No. 12 26
Alternate Picking Exercise No. 13 26
Alternate Picking Exercise No. 14 27
Alternate Picking Exercise No. 15 27
Alternate Picking Exercise No. 16 28
Alternate Picking Exercise No. 17 28

Chapter 6 Hammer-ons and Pull-offs
Hammer-ons and Pull-offs 29
Hammer-on Pull-off Exercise No. 1 30
Hammer-on Pull-off Exercise No. 2 31
Hammer-on Pull-off Exercise No. 3 32
Hammer-on Pull-off Exercise No. 4 32
Hammer-on Pull-off Exercise No. 5 33
Hammer-on Pull-off Exercise No. 6 33

Hammer-on Pull-off Exercise No. 7 34
Hammer-on Pull-off Exercise No. 8 34
Hammer-on Pull-off Exercise No. 9 35
Hammer-on Pull-off Exercise No. 10 36
Hammer-on Pull-off Exercise No. 11 36
Hammer-on Pull-off Exercise No. 12 36
Hammer-on Pull-off Exercise No. 13 37
Hammer-on Pull-off Exercise No. 14 37
Hammer-on Pull-off Exercise No. 15 38
Hammer-on Pull-off Exercise No. 16 38
Hammer-on Pull-off Exercise No. 17 39
Hammer-on Pull-off Exercise No. 18 39

Chapter 7 Putting it Together

Jesu, Joy of Man's Desiring 40
Brandenburg Concerto No. 5 41
Sailor's Hornpipe 42
The Devil's Dream 43
Concerto Grosso No. 10 44
Sonata No. 11 45
Symphony No. 29 46

About the Author

Don J. MacLean is an active freelance guitarist, composer and educator. His musical training includes studies at the Royal Conservatory of Music, Humber College, and York University, where he obtained his B.A. (Dbl. Hons. Maj.) in music and psychology. His twenty years of teaching, performing and composing have made Don a highly sought-after expert for workshops, seminars and master classes.

Don J. MacLean is the author of:

The World of Scales: A Compendium of Scales for the Modern Guitar Player
The World of Scales: A Compendium of Scales for all Instruments

Guitar Essentials: Chord Master
Guitar Essentials: Chord Master Expanded Edition
Guitar Essentials: Scale Master 1
Guitar Essentials: Scale Master Expanded Edition
Guitar Essentials: Improviser
Guitar Essentials: Chord and Scale Master Series

Music Essentials: Improviser

Absolute Essentials of Music Theory
Absolute Essentials of Guitar

Fit Fingers Book 1
Fit Fingers Book 2

Quick Tips for Faster Fingers
Quick Tips: Guitar Technique 101
Quick Tips: Guitar Chords 101
Quick Tips: Guitar Scales 101

Mega Chops: Mozart for Pick-Style Guitar
Mega Chops: Bach for Pick-Style Guitar
Mega Chops: Corelli for Pick-Style Guitar
Mega Chops: Vivaldi for Pick-Style Guitar

Introduction

Welcome to Quick Tips: Guitar Technique 101. This book contains 36 exercises and 7 pieces, that will improve the technique of the beginner to intermediate guitar player.

One of the most frequent questions I am asked by my students is: "How can I improve my technique?" The answer to this question is: practice, practice, practice. The more time you spend on the guitar, the better you will get. What you practice and how you practice, determines your level of accomplishment. Practicing the exercises in this book will make you a better player. Depending on your playing goals, you should spend anywhere from ten to sixty minutes a day working on these exercises.

The examples that appear in this book are excerpts from Quick Tips for Faster Fingers and Fit Fingers Books 1&2, which will provide you with further techniques, studies and pieces.

Chapter 1

Basics

How to Hold the Guitar

The best way for a right-handed player to hold the guitar, is to position the guitar on the left leg. The right leg should be used for the left-handed guitarist. This may feel uncomfortable at first, but positioning the guitar on the appropriate leg will make it easier for you to stretch your fingers.

OK

Best

How to Hold a Pick

Guitar picks or plectrums, come in a wide variety of shapes and sizes. It is best to use either a medium or heavy pick. Thin picks flop around too much and will slow you down. The pick should be held between the thumb and the first finger as shown on the following page.

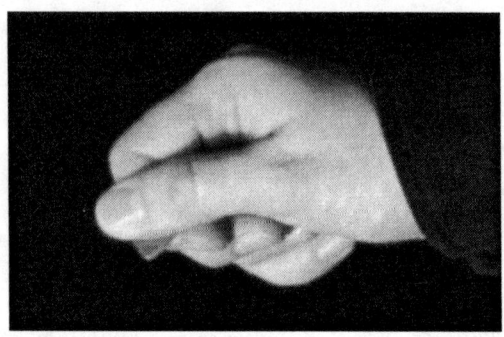

When you play the guitar you will either pick an individual string or strum several simultaneously. You should use only the very tip of the pick to strike the string.

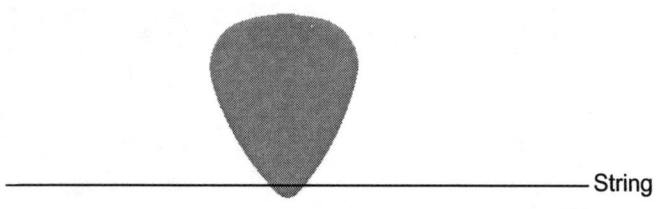 String

Front View.

View from Bottom.

Top-down View.

In order to lessen the confusion between left and right-handed guitar players, the term fret-hand will be used to denote the actual hand you use to play any notes on the neck of the guitar. Your fret-hand fingers are numbered accordingly:

The thumb is generally not used to play notes.

Fret-hand Position

To produce clear notes it is necessary to maintain proper hand positioning. The palm of your hand should not make contact with the neck of the guitar—use only the tips of your fret-hand fingers. Position the fingers as close as possible to the metal fret wire. Placing your finger on top of the fret wire will produce a muffled note. Your thumb should be placed on the back of the neck in line with your second or third finger. When your hand is in proper position, a thick highlighter will fit between your palm and the neck of the guitar.

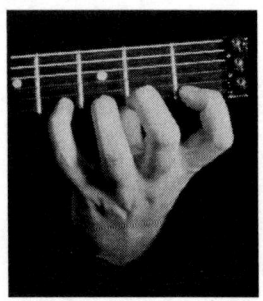
Front View.

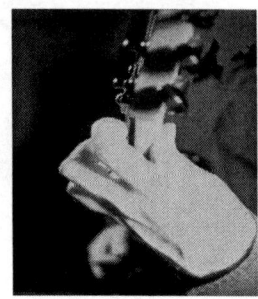
Side View.

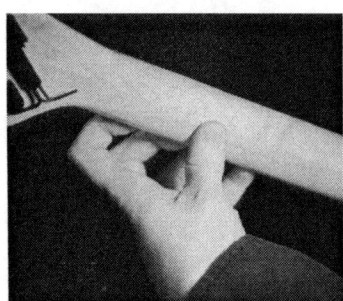
Rear View.

View from Bottom.

Note that there is enough space to fit a highlighter between the palm and the neck.

Music Notation

Guitar music can be notated in four different ways: standard notation, tablature, rhythm/slash notation and neck diagrams or grids. This book uses only standard notation and tablature.

Standard Notation

Standard notation indicates the pitch of a note and also its duration. In standard notation the first symbol you will encounter is called a clef. A clef is a symbol used to indicate the pitch of a particular line. Guitar music is written in the treble clef. The treble clef is sometimes called the "G" clef because it indicates the position of the note G. The musical alphabet consists of the first seven letters of the alphabet: A—B—C—D—E—F—G. An easy way to remember the notes in the treble clef is to use the following mnemonics:

Every Good Boy Deserves Fudge (notes on lines)

FACE (notes in spaces)

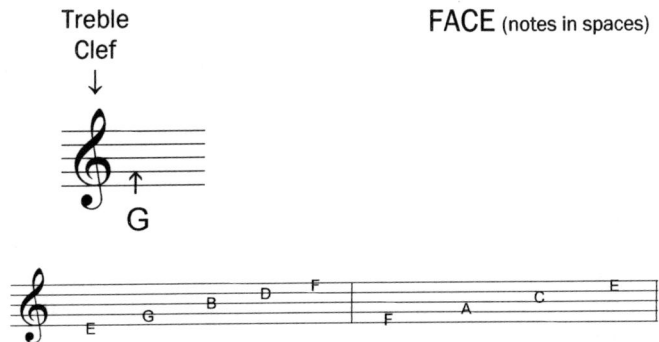

A Quick Overview of Tablature

In tablature, each horizontal line represents a string. The strings are numbered from the thinnest (1) to the thickest (6). The numbers on these lines represent the frets that you need to place your fingers on.

Chapter 2
Rhythm

Meter

Music is usually organized in a repeatable accent pattern known as meter. The repeatable accent pattern will consist of a combination of strong and weak beats. For example:

2/4 time consists of: (S= strong, W= weak)
    S   W

3/4 time consists of:
    S   W   W

4/4 time consists of:
    S   W   M   W (M stands for medium weak)

5/4 time consists of:
    S   W   S   W   W

    or
    S   W   W   S   W

S W M W   S W W   S W S W W *or:* S W W S W

Time Values

The most common time signature, 4/4, (pronounced four-four) is often abbreviated with a fancy "C" and called common time. In 4/4, the whole note receives four beats or counts. The half note receives two beats and the quarter note receives one beat. Eighth notes each receive half of a beat.

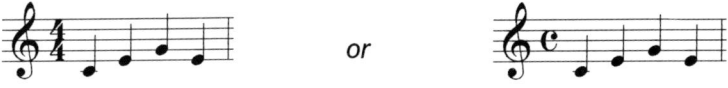

Note Durations

Eighth notes are sometimes written without connecting beams:

The whole note receives 4 beats; the half note receives 2 beats; a quarter note receives 1 beat and an eighth note receives 1/2 of a beat; a sixteenth note receives 1/4 of a beat and the triplet receives 1/3 of a beat.

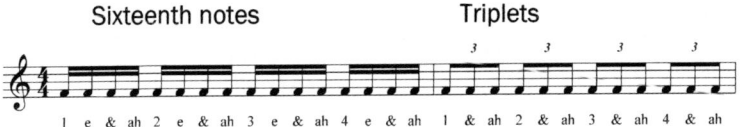

Rest Durations

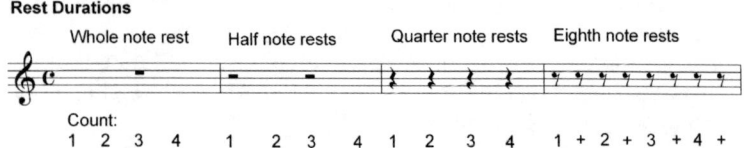

Time Signatures

A time signature is used to indicate the strong and weak beats in a measure and also which note value receives one beat. In Simple Time (2/2, 2/4, 2/8, 3/2, 3/4, 3/8, 4/2, 4/4, 4/8), the top number of the time signature indicates the number of beats per measure while the bottom number indicates the type of note that receives one beat. For example:

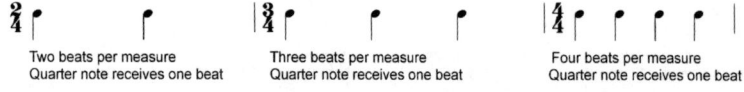

In Simple Time you tap your foot on each beat. In Compound Time, (6/4, 6/8, 6/16, 9/4, 9/8, 9/16, 12/4, 12/8, 12/16) you should tap your foot on each major beat division. In 6/8 time the measure is divided into two (1 2 3), (4 5 6). Nine-eight time has three main divisions (1 2 3), (4 5 6), (7 8 9). Twelve-eight time contains 4 main divisions (1 2 3), (4 5 6), (7 8 9), (10 11 12). In 6/8, you would count 1 2 3 4 5 6, but only tap your foot on 1 and 4. In 9/8, you would count 1 2 3 4 5 6 7 8 9, and tap your foot on 1, 4 and 7. In 12/8 time, you count 1 2 3 4 5 6 7 8 9 10 11 12, and tap your foot on 1, 4, 7 and 10.

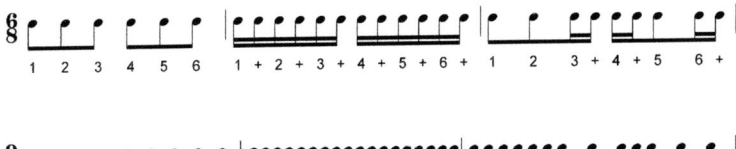

Dotted and Tied Notes

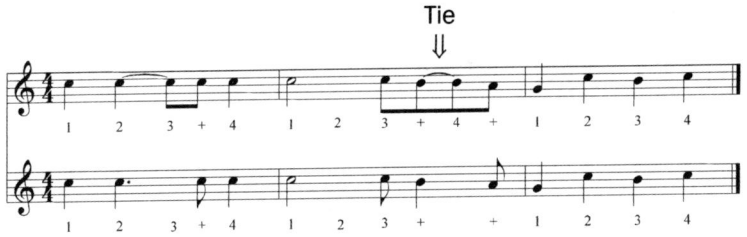

Ties and dots are used to increase the time value of the notes they follow. A dot increases the time value of a note by half. A half note receives 2 beats; a dotted half note receives 3 beats. A quarter note receives one beat; a dotted quarter note receives one and a half beats. An eighth note receives half of a beat; a dotted eighth note receives half of a beat plus one quarter of a beat (in other words 3/4's of a beat).

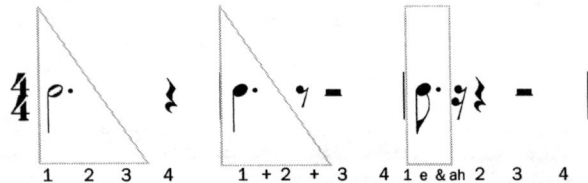

The notes in a tie are of the same pitch. A tie increases the time value of a note by the value of the second note. You do not pick the second note of the tie. You simply sustain the note for the duration of the first note plus the value of the note it is tied to.

Repeats
Instead of writing out the same music twice, repeats are used.

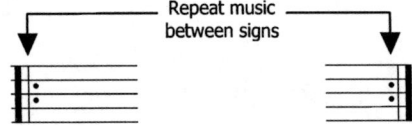

Chapter 3

How to Practice

Consistency is one of the most important variables that will allow you to achieve your guitar goals. Our muscles and nervous system are able to adapt quickly to repeated demands placed on them. The key here, is that the demands must be made repeatedly for the body to adapt. You are not going to get stronger by lifting weights only once. To get strong you need to workout consistently with an intelligent program. The same is true for music—your muscles and fingertips have to adapt to the demands being placed on them so that new and more efficient neural pathways can be formed. This is easily accomplished by playing everyday with an intelligent program. You will progress at a faster rate if you practice thirty minutes each day as opposed to playing for an hour every other day.

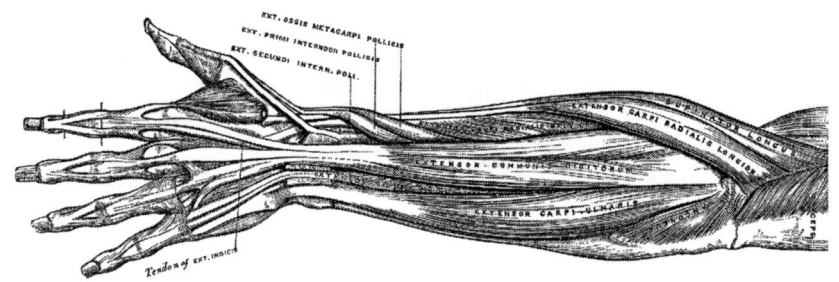

Once you determine the amount of time you can practice each day, take that time and divide it in half. To increase your technical ability, the first half of your practice session should be spent performing exercises, scales, arpeggios, etc., and the second half devoted to application. By application, I am referring to the reason you originally picked up the instrument—to play songs. It is very important that you divide your time up this way. Let's say you have a half an hour per day that you can devote to playing the guitar. The first fifteen minutes should be spent on technique building exercises and the last fifteen minutes should be devoted to practicing and learning new songs. The reason you should do it this way, is because it is very easy to get lost in the songs and lose track of time. If you practice the songs first, you will usually find that your half hour is up and you didn't play a single technique exercise. Also, practicing your scales, chords and warm-up exercises first, will allow you to warm-up—making it easier to play the songs that follow. If more time materializes in the day, you can either repeat the cycle, or consider it free time and play whatever you want.

The pieces presented in this book should be included in the technique/warm-up portion of your practice session. If you are relatively new to the guitar, the best approach is to take one exercise from each chapter and practice them each day for a week. At the start of the new week, start on one new exercise from each chapter.

If you are an intermediate player you should practice two or more exercises from each chapter every week. As your technique improves, so will your speed. This means that you will be able to play more exercises in your practice session and therefore accomplish more.

If you practice these exercises everyday, you will hear the results in a very short period of time. Also, you will notice that your pick-hand and fret-hand will *feel* different. Your fret-hand will get stronger and your accuracy with a pick will dramatically improve.

Chapter 4

Vibrato

To add variety and a bit of colour to notes, you will find vibrato to be an indispensable technique. In vibrato, you take a note and slightly pull it sharp and then return it to its original pitch. This process is repeated several times. Depending on the desired effect this can be done slowly or rapidly.

There are two main types of vibrato. The most common form used in rock, pop, folk, country and blues is performed by moving the fret-hand finger up and down in relation to the string. In essence, you are moving your finger perpendicular to the string. Some guitarists favour a subtle vibrato where the note is only moved slightly. Others prefer to employ a wide vibrato in which the string is moved aggressively up and down. A second type of vibrato that is used by classical guitarists is performed parallel to the string. To perform this type of vibrato you must play the note in the middle of the fret and then rock your finger side-to-side along the length of the string.

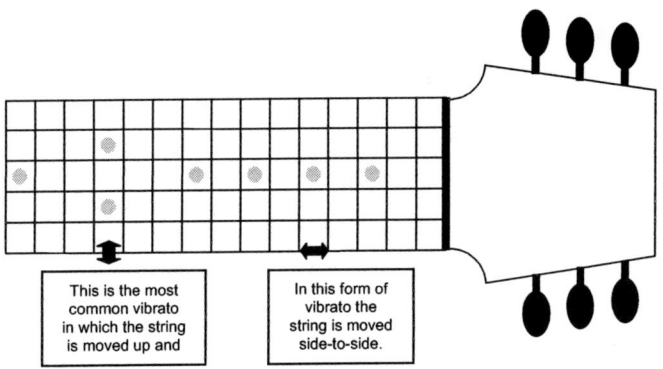

This is the most common vibrato in which the string is moved up and down.

In this form of vibrato the string is moved side-to-side.

Unless it is quite pronounced, vibrato is not symbolized in sheet music. The reason for this is that it is assumed that the guitarist will add vibrato where appropriate. Generally, you will find that vibrato will be used on most notes that have a duration of a quarter note or longer. Depending on the tempo of the song you may use vibrato on eighth and even sixteenth notes. When it is symbolized, vibrato is denoted as:

Vibrato Exercise # 1
Practice this exercise with both types of vibrato.

Chapter 5

Alternate Picking

Alternate picking is the most common and efficient way to play notes on individual strings. When you learn to play new songs, you can safely assume that alternate picking should be used. Alternate picking requires that you strike the first note with a down-stroke (⊓) and the next note with an up-stroke (v). The pattern is repeated for each successive note.

Here is how to play the first alternate picking exercise that follows. To start the exercise, begin on the first string, 1st fret. The number combination 1-2-3-4, represents your fret-hand fingers. Remember that your fret-hand fingers are numbered from one to four (index to pinky). To play this exercise, place your first finger on the 1st fret and pick the note. Next, place your second finger on the 2nd fret and strike this note. Place your third finger on the third fret and play this note. Finally, position your fourth finger on the fourth fret and pick this note. You are now ready to repeat this pattern starting on the second fret. The exercise 1-2-3-4, should be repeated on each fret until your fourth finger reaches the twelfth fret. You then play the exercise backwards (4-3-2-1) to the 1st fret. This exercise should be practiced on two or more strings every day.

⊓   Down-Stroke

V   Up-Stroke

Alternate Picking Exercise # 1

1234
Ascending

Continue up to the 12th fret

Descending

Continue down to the first fret

Alternate Picking Exercise # 2

1243
Ascending

Continue up to the 12th fret

Descending

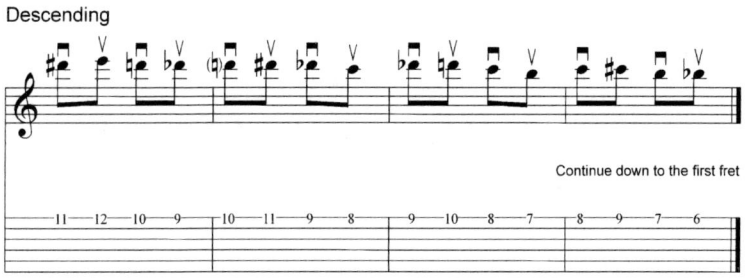

Continue down to the first fret

Alternate Picking Exercise # 3

1324
Ascending

Descending

Alternate Picking Exercise # 4

1342
Ascending

Descending

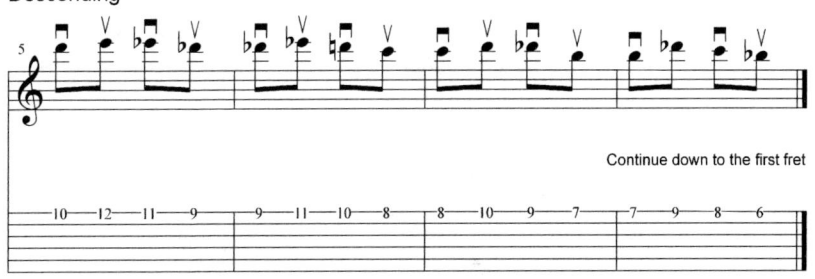

Alternate Picking Exercise # 5

1432
Ascending

Continue up to the 12th fret

Descending

Continue down to the first fret

Alternate Picking Exercise # 6

1423
Ascending

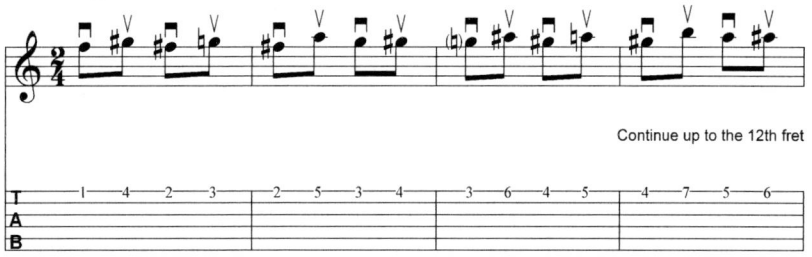

Continue up to the 12th fret

Descending

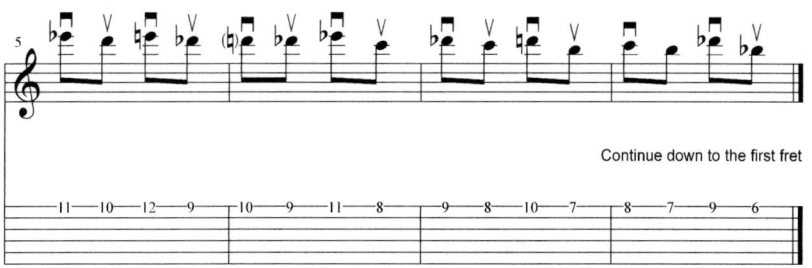

Continue down to the first fret

Alternate Picking Exercise # 7

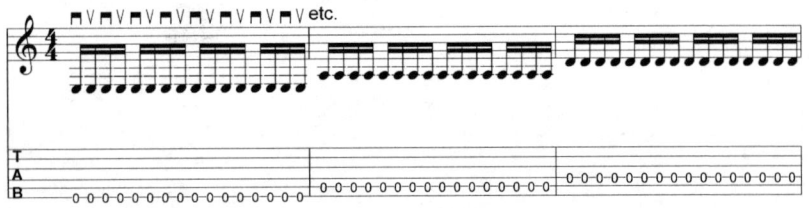

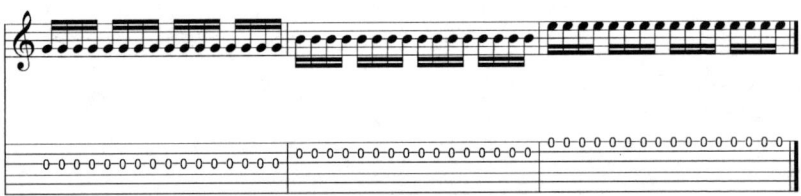

Alternate Picking Exercise # 8

You should also play the first six alternate picking exercises across the fretboard. Instead of ascending and descending up one string at a time, you can play the finger combination on the first fret, sixth string, then repeat the pattern on the fifth string first fret, etc. Practice the exercise on each fret ascending and descending.

Ascending

Descending

Repeat pattern starting on the second fret.

Alternate Picking Exercise # 9
C Major Scale Fingering 1
Scales are an excellent way to develop picking dexterity. The first note is played with a down-stroke and the second is played with an up-stroke. Continue this pattern with each successive note.

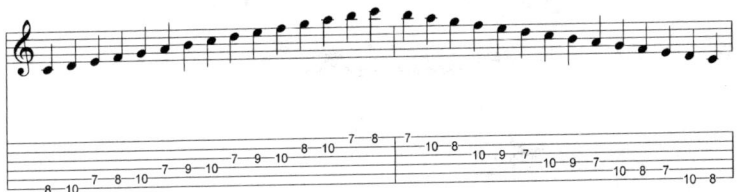

Alternate Picking Exercise # 10
C Major Scale Fingering 2
Here is a second way to play the C major scale.

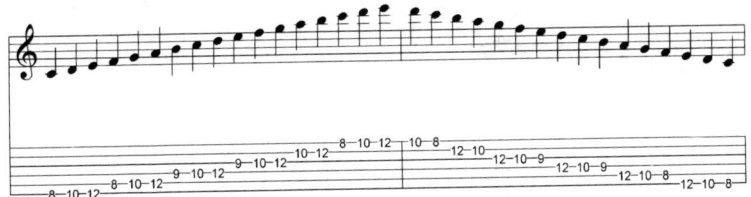

Alternate Picking Exercise # 11
A Minor Scale

Alternate Picking Exercise # 12
A Minor Pentatonic Scale

Alternate Picking Exercise # 13
C Major Pentatonic Scale

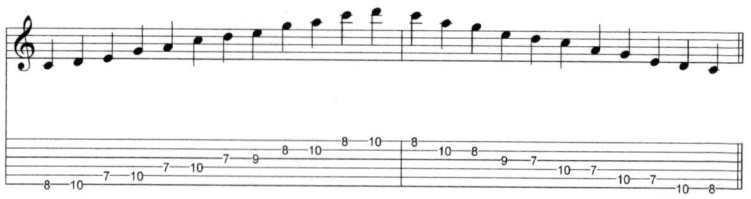

Alternate Picking Exercise # 14
A Harmonic Minor Scale

Alternate Picking Exercise # 15
C Major Scale in Thirds

Alternate Picking Exercise # 16
A Minor Scale in Thirds

Alternate Picking Exercise # 17
A Harmonic Minor Scale in Thirds

Chapter 6

Hammer-ons and Pull-offs

In some contexts, you want to play notes that sound fluid. The term for this is legato. The best way to play notes in a legato fashion is to use hammer-ons and/or pull-offs. A hammer-on is produced by striking the lower pitched note and then sounding the higher note with your fret-hand. You do not pick the note that is hammered. The pull-off is the opposite of the hammer-on. To perform a pull-off you pick the higher pitched note and then sound the lower note with your fret-hand. Place both fingers on the notes to be sounded and then pull-off the higher finger so that the lower note is heard. You do not pick the note that is pulled off.

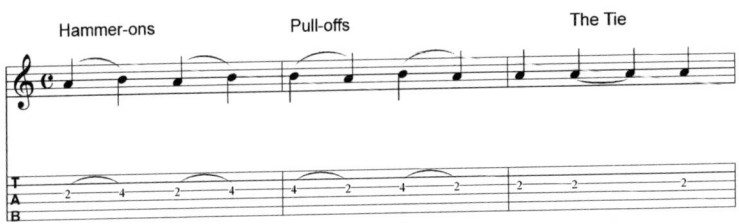

Keep in mind that the curved line used to symbolize a hammer-on or pull-off is also used for a tie. The notes in a tie are of the same pitch. A tie increases the time value of a note by the value of the second note. As you can see in the tablature above, you do not pick the second note of the tie. The first note of the tie is held for the duration of the two notes combined.

Quick Tips: Guitar Technique 101

Hammer-on Pull-off Exercise # 1

Pick the first note on each string and hammer-on the rest. Play the descending version of the exercise by picking the first note on the string and sound the remaining notes with pull-offs. Practice exercise 1 on each fret up to the 12th fret. Once you reach the twelfth fret play the entire exercise backwards to the first fret. This is a great endurance exercise—if your hands get fatigued, just play the exercise up to the 7th fret. Every week our so, make it your goal to add one or more additional frets. Hammer-on and pull-off exercises 1-5 should be performed on each fret and played to the 12th fret.

Hammer-on Pull-off Exercise # 2

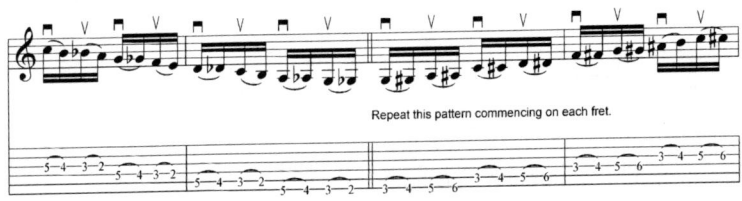

Hammer-on Pull-off Exercise # 3
Finger combo 1-2. Repeat this exercise on each fret up to the 12th fret.

Hammer-on Pull-off Exercise # 4
Finger combo 1-3. Repeat this exercise on each fret up to the 12th fret.

Hammer-on Pull-off Exercise # 5

Finger combo 1-4. Repeat this exercise on each fret up to the 12th fret.

Hammer-on Pull-off Exercise # 6

Finger combo 2-3. Repeat this exercise on each fret up to the 12th fret.

Hammer-on Pull-off Exercise # 7

Finger combo 2-4. Repeat this exercise on each fret up to the 12th fret.

Hammer-on Pull-off Exercise # 8

Finger combo 3-4. Repeat this exercise on each fret up to the 12th fret.

Hammer-on Pull-off Exercise # 9

Finger combo 1-2, 2-3, 3-4. What is shown below is one cycle through the exercise. The entire pattern should be repeated on each fret up to the 12th fret. To turn this exercise into a great endurance test, pick only the first note on each string. The rest of the notes should be played as hammer-ons or pull-offs.

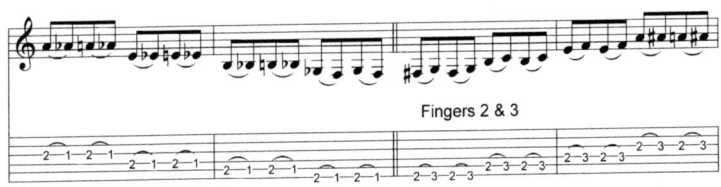

Quick Tips: Guitar Technique 101

Hammer-on Pull-off Exercise # 10
Finger combo 1-2-3 and 2-3-4
In addition to playing this exercise with fingers 1-2-3, you should also play it using fingers 2-3-4. Remember that you are only picking the first note on each string.

Hammer-on Pull-off Exercise # 11
Finger combo 1-2-4

Hammer-on Pull-off Exercise # 12
Finger combo 1-3-4

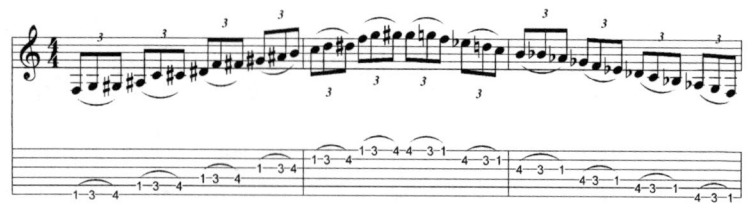

Hammer-on Pull-off Exercise # 13

Finger combo 1-4. Open string pull-offs. Also try picking only the first note in each measure. All of the remaining notes should be played as hammer-ons and or pull-offs.

Hammer-on Pull-off Exercise # 14

Finger combo 1-4. Open string pull-offs with a bit of a stretch.

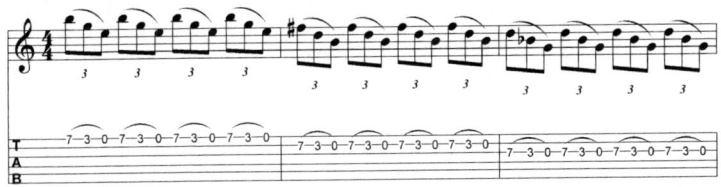

Hammer-on Pull-off Exercise # 15

E minor pentatonic. You should also practice scales with hammer-ons and pull-offs.

Hammer-on Pull-off Exercise # 16

C Major

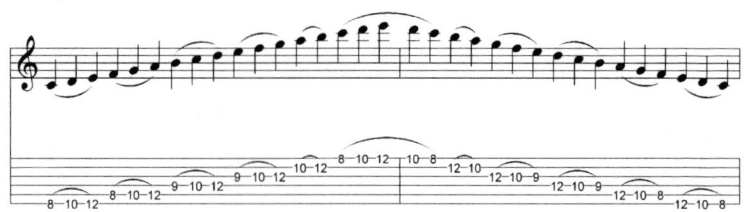

Hammer-on Pull-off Exercise # 17
A Minor

Hammer-on Pull-off Exercise # 18
A Minor Pentatonic

Chapter 7

Putting it Together

This final chapter will provide you with some actual pieces that will allow you to practice the techniques presented in this book. Enjoy!

JESU, JOY OF MAN'S DESIRING

J.S. Bach
Arr. by Don J. MacLean

Brandenburg Concerto No. 5 in D Major
1st Movement Excerpt

J.S. Bach
Arr. by Don J. MacLean

Sailor's Hornpipe

Arr. by: Don J. MacLean

THE DEVIL'S DREAM

Arr. by Don J. MacLean

Concerto Grosso No. 10
Allemanda

A. Corelli
Arr. by Don J. MacLean

Sonata No. 11
Gavotta

A. Corelli
Arr. by Don J. MacLean

© 2003 Agogic Publishing   All Rights Reserved   International Copyright Secured

Symphony No. 29
A Major Excerpt

W.A. Mozart
Arr. by Don J. MacLean

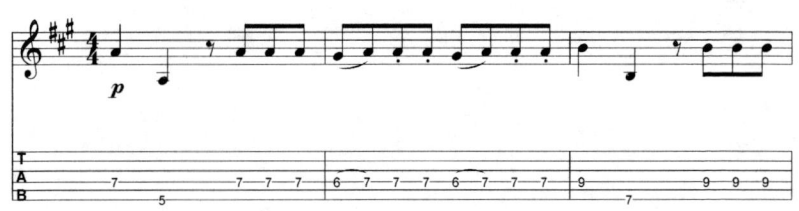

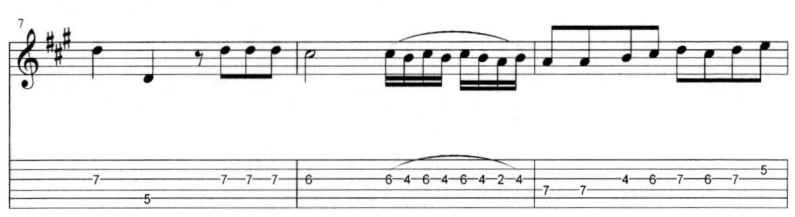

Quick Tips: Guitar Technique 101

Available from
AGOGIC PUBLISHING

QUICK TIPS FOR FASTER FINGERS
Wouldn't you rather play faster, more accurately and with better technique? Add a new dimension to your guitar playing with 54 specially chosen and created technique builders for massive chops. Whether you are a beginner or intermediate guitar player, you will refer to this text again and again. Includes audio CD.
ISBN 1-896595-10-3
$22.95 CDN $17.95 USD
62 pages, 8.5 X 11
Book and Audio CD
Author: Don J. MacLean

QUICK TIPS: GUITAR TECHNIQUE 101
Quick Tips: Guitar Technique 101, contains 36 specially created exercises and 7 pieces for massive chops. This book shows you foundation exercises that will increase your speed, strength and accuracy.
ISBN 1-896595-25-1
$9.99
52 pages, 5.5 X 8.5
Author: Don J. MacLean

QUICK TIPS: GUITAR CHORDS 101
Don't let the compact size fool you! *Quick Tips Guitar Chords 101,* will show you all the essential guitar chords you need to play your favourite songs. Discover how easy it is to play: basic chords, power chords, barre chords, and basic chord progressions.
ISBN 1-896595-27-8
$9.99
60 pages, 5.5 X 8.5
Author: Don J. MacLean

ABSOLUTE ESSENTIALS OF MUSIC THEORY
Just what you absolutely need to know! In this easy-to-follow self-study guide, are all the need-to-know basics, demystified, chapter by chapter. Discover how easy it is to understand: music notation, scales, intervals, chords, harmonized scales, and rhythm. For all instruments, beginner to intermediate. Answer key included.
ISBN 1-896595-12-X
$19.99
69 pages, 8.5 X 11
Author: Don J. MacLean

WORLD OF SCALES: A COMPENDIUM OF SCALES FOR THE MODERN GUITAR PLAYER

THE WORLD OF SCALES: A COMPENDIUM OF SCALES FOR THE MODERN GUITAR PLAYER shows guitarists of all levels how scales can be used. The World of Scales provides the reader with the most comprehensive examination of scales available. All scales are shown in easy-to-read and transposable fingerings.

ISBN 1-896595-07-3
$25.95 CDN $19.95 USD
165 pages, 8.5 X 11
Author: Don J. MacLean
Editor: Rob Bowman Ph.D.

WORLD OF SCALES: A COMPENDIUM OF SCALES FOR ALL INSTRUMENTS 2ND EDITION

THE WORLD OF SCALES: A COMPENDIUM OF SCALES FOR ALL INSTRUMENTS enables intermediate to advanced musicians to understand: how scales are built; how chords are constructed and interact with scales; and how to apply modalization to any scale. The World of Scales provides the reader with the most thorough examination of scales available. All scales are shown in treble and bass clefs.

ISBN 1-896595-21-9
$25.95 CDN $19.95 USD
96 pages, 8.5 X 11
Author: Don J. MacLean

GUITAR ESSENTIALS: SCALE MASTER EXPANDED EDITION

The key to 1004 scales! With GUITAR ESSENTIALS: SCALE MASTER EXPANDED EDITION you will discover how easy it is to master scales. Learn 16 scale types with 92 fingerings transposed to all keys for a total of 1004 scales. This expanded edition provides you with tips and short-cuts that make learning scales a snap. Scales have never made more sense.

ISBN 1-896595-26-X
$19.99
75 pages; 8.5 X 11
Author: Don J. MacLean

GUITAR ESSENTIALS: CHORD MASTER EXPANDED EDITION

Make an instant impact on your playing with GUITAR ESSENTIALS: CHORD MASTER EXPANDED EDITION. Loaded with new features, this expanded edition is easy-to-understand and perfect for all styles of music. Learn how to play 36 basic chords and 95 moveable chords in all 12 keys, for a total of 1176 chords.

ISBN 1-896595-24-3
$17.99
51 pages; 8.5 X 11
Author: Don J. MacLean

MUSIC ESSENTIALS: IMPROVISER

Laminated Reference Chart
MUSIC ESSENTIALS: IMPROVISER provides the intermediate musician with the tools to improvise over chords. Start with a scale and view the chords that can be used or, select a chord and view its scale options. All scales are shown in treble and bass clefs. The Improviser is the first chart to provide musicians with easy access to this information and is the perfect companion to *The World of Scales*.

ISBN 1-896595-23-5
$7.99 CDN $6.99 USD
1 Double sided page; 11 X 17
Blue and silver

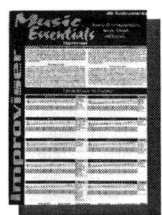

GUITAR ESSENTIALS: IMPROVISER

Laminated Reference Chart
GUITAR ESSENTIALS: IMPROVISER provides the intermediate guitarist with the tools to improvise over chords. Start with a scale and view the chords that can be used or, select a chord and view its scale options. All scale forms are shown in transposable neck diagrams. The Improviser is the first chart to provide guitar players with easy access to this information and is the perfect companion to *The World of Scales*.

ISBN 1-896595-19-7
$7.99 CDN $6.99 USD
1 Double sided page; 11 X 17
Black and gold

GUITAR ESSENTIALS: CHORD MASTER

Laminated Reference Chart
GUITAR ESSENTIALS: THE CHORD MASTER shows guitarists of all levels how to quickly and easily play 1176 of the most common guitar chords. This is the ultimate guitar chord cheat-sheet!

ISBN 1-896595-13-8
$4.99
1 Double sided page; 8½ X 11
Black and red

GUITAR ESSENTIALS: SCALE MASTER 1

Laminated Reference Chart
GUITAR ESSENTIALS: THE SCALE MASTER 1 shows you how to play the most common scales. Major, minor, harmonic minor, melodic minor, major pentatonic, minor pentatonic, blues and the composite blues scales are all included in this chart.

ISBN 1-896595-11-1
$4.99 CDN $3.99 USD
1 Double sided page; 8½ X 11
Black and red

CHECK YOUR LEADING BOOK/MUSIC STORE
OR VISIT US ONLINE @ www.agogic.biz

ORDER FORM

Buy 2 or more products and receive *FREE* shipping!!!

Canadian Order Form

Free shipping when you buy 2 or more titles

Prices shown in Canadian dollars	Price	Shipping	GST	TOTAL	Qty.
World of Scales for Guitar	$ 25.95	free	$ 1.82	$ 27.77	
World of Scales for all Inst	$ 25.95	free	$ 1.82	$ 27.77	
Guitar Essentials: Chord Master	$ 4.99	free	$ 0.35	$ 5.34	
Guitar Essentials: Scale Master 1	$ 4.99	free	$ 0.35	$ 5.34	
Guitar Essentials: Improviser	$ 7.99	free	$ 0.56	$ 8.55	
Music Essentials: Improviser	$ 7.99	free	$ 0.56	$ 8.55	
Guitar Essentials: Chord Master Exp Ed	$ 17.99	free	$ 1.26	$ 19.25	
Guitar Essentials: Scale Master Exp Ed	$ 19.99	free	$ 1.40	$ 21.39	
Absolute Essentials of Music Theory	$ 19.99	free	$ 1.40	$ 21.39	
Quick Tips for Faster Fingers	$ 22.95	free	$ 1.61	$ 24.56	
Quick Tips: Guitar Technique 101	$ 9.99	free	$ 0.70	$ 10.69	
Quick Tips: Guitar Chords 101	$ 9.99	free	$ 0.70	$ 10.69	
QTT101				**TOTAL**	
To order an individual title, please add $5.00 for shipping plus G.S.T.				**Qty.**	

Ship To:

Name _____

Address _____

City/ Prov/State _____

Postal/Zip Code _____

Phone _____

Email _____

Mail this order form today with your money order payable to:

Agogic Publishing

406-109 Tenth Street
New Westminster, BC
V3M 3X7
Phone 604-290-2692
Fax 604-540-4419

CHECK YOUR LEADING BOOK/MUSIC STORE
OR VISIT US ONLINE @ www.agogic.biz

ORDER FORM
Buy 2 or more products and receive FREE shipping!!!

U.S. Order Form
Free shipping when you buy 2 or more titles

Prices shown in U.S. dollars	Price	Shipping	TOTAL	Qty.
World of Scales for Guitar	$ 19.95	free	$19.95	
World of Scales for all Inst	$ 19.95	free	$19.95	
Guitar Essentials: Chord Master	$ 4.99	free	$ 4.99	
Guitar Essentials: Scale Master 1	$ 3.99	free	$ 3.99	
Guitar Essentials: Improviser	$ 6.99	free	$ 6.99	
Music Essentials: Improviser	$ 6.99	free	$ 6.99	
Guitar Essentials: Chord Master Exp Ed	$ 17.99	free	$17.99	
Guitar Essentials: Scale Master Exp Ed	$ 19.99	free	$19.99	
Absolute Essentials of Music Theory	$ 19.99	free	$19.99	
Quick Tips for Faster Fingers	$ 17.95	free	$17.95	
Quick Tips: Guitar Technique 101	$ 9.99	free	$ 9.99	
Quick Tips: Guitar Chords 101	$ 9.99	free	$ 9.99	

To order an individual title, please add $5.00 for shipping

TOTAL Qty.

Ship To:
Name _____
Address _____
City/State _____
Zip Code _____
Phone _____
Email _____

Mail this order form today with your money order payable to:

Agogic Publishing
406-109 Tenth Street
New Westminster, BC
V3M 3X7
Phone 604-290-2692
Fax 604-540-4419

Notes